Alexander Graham Bell

A Photo-Illustrated Biography
by Greg Linder

Consultant:
Judith Tulloch
Historian, Parks Canada
Alexander Graham Bell National Historic Site

Bridgestone Books

an imprint of Capstone Press
Mankato, Minnesota

Bridgestone Books are published by Capstone Press
818 North Willow Street, Mankato, Minnesota 56001
http://www.capstone-press.com

Library of Congress Cataloging-in-Publication Data
Linder, Greg, 1950–
    Alexander Graham Bell: a photo-illustrated biography/by Greg Linder.
    p. cm.—(Photo-illustrated biographies)
    Includes bibliographical references and index.
    Summary: A biography of the inventor and teacher of the deaf, who experimented in many
areas, including electricity, giant kites, and boats called hydrofoils, and became famous for
inventing the telephone.
    ISBN 0-7368-0202-9
    1. Bell, Alexander Graham, 1847–1922—Juvenile literature. 2. Bell, Alexander Graham,
1847–1922—Pictorial works—Juvenile literature. 3. Inventors—United States—Biography—
Juvenile literature. [1. Bell, Alexander Graham, 1847–1922. 2. Inventors.] I. Title. II. Series.
TK6143.B4L55 1999
621.385′092—dc21
[B]   98-31474
                                                                                                    CIP
                                                                                                    AC

Editorial Credits
Chuck Miller, editor; Timothy Halldin, cover designer; Kimberly Danger, photo researcher

Photo Credits
Archive Photos, cover
Corbis-Bettman, 4, 10, 12, 14, 18, 20
Parks Canada (Alexander Graham Bell National Historic Site), 6, 8; (Susan Tooke, artist), 16

Table of Contents

"We are all too inclined, I think, to walk through life with our eyes shut. There are things all around us, and right at our very feet, that we have never seen; because we never really looked."
—Alec in a speech to graduates of the Friends School in Washington, D.C., 1914

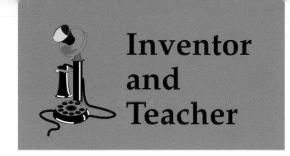

Inventor and Teacher

Alexander Graham Bell was a famous inventor. He is best known for inventing the telephone.

Alec invented the telephone in 1876. His invention changed the way people communicate. Alec's telephone let people talk with each other over long distances. Alec later started a telephone company with several business partners. Today, the telephone company is known as AT&T.

Alec produced many other inventions. He made giant kites that lifted people into the air. He built a boat called a hydrofoil. The hydrofoil traveled above the water. It once was the world's fastest boat.

Alec started his career as a speech teacher. He taught students who were deaf how to speak. He also taught them how to understand what people were saying. Alec helped people with hearing problems throughout his life.

The invention of the telephone made Alec a wealthy man. This allowed him to devote his life to further inventions.

Life in Scotland

Alec was born March 3, 1847, in Edinburgh, Scotland. His parents did not give him a middle name. He chose Graham when he was 10 because he liked it. But most people called him Alec.

Alec's father was Alexander Melville Bell. People called him by his middle name. Melville was a speech teacher. He taught his students to speak words correctly.

Alec's mother was Eliza Bell. She was an artist. She painted pictures of people. Eliza also was a skilled piano player.

Eliza taught Alec and his two brothers, Edward and Melville, at home. The boys learned reading, writing, math, and art. Eliza also taught them to play the piano.

Alec was a talented piano player like his mother. As a young man, Alec planned to become a musician.

Melville and Eliza had three sons, Alec (far left), Melville Jr. (center), and Edward (not pictured).

The Study of Speech

In 1863, Alec was in London, England, with his father. He saw a speaking machine built by Sir Charles Wheatstone. Sir Charles could make his machine pronounce a few simple words.

Alec and his brother Melville decided to build a speaking machine. They used tin and rubber. They shaped a head, teeth, tongue, mouth, and throat. Their machine said "Ma-Ma!" in a high voice. Neighbors thought the noise was from a baby.

Later, Alec experimented with the family dog. The dog was a terrier named Trouve. Alec taught Trouve to growl on command. Alec carefully moved the dog's mouth and throat as it growled. Trouve seemed to talk.

Alec's friends and neighbors laughed at these experiments. But such experiments sparked Alec's lifelong interest in sound and speech.

Alec's experiments with his dog sparked his interest in sound and speech. Both his father and grandfather were speech teachers.

"Speech is a mere motion of air."
–Alec in a speech to the
National Convention of Deaf School Principals, 1872

Teacher of the Deaf

Alec started to think about the problems faced by people who are deaf. Eliza was nearly deaf. Alec's father, Melville, taught students who were deaf.

Alec finished high school when he was 15 years old. In 1863, he started his first job as a speech and music teacher in Scotland. Later, Alec taught in England and the United States.

Alec's father had invented visible speech. This teaching method used pictures to show students how to make sounds.

Most people thought those who were deaf could not learn to speak. But Alec used visible speech to teach his students who were deaf.

Alec also taught his students to read lips. They watched the way people's lips moved to understand what was said. Alec's students learned to both speak and listen.

Alec helped Helen Keller learn to speak. Helen was deaf and blind. She became a famous author and public speaker.

The Move to America

Alec's brother Edward died of tuberculosis in 1867. His brother Melville died of the same lung disease in 1870. Alec's parents were afraid Alec would become sick too.

The Bells decided to move away from Scotland. Alec's father thought the wet climate was unhealthy. The Bells sailed to Canada in July of 1870. The family bought a farm in Ontario.

Alec moved to Boston, Massachusetts, in 1871. He taught speech to students who were deaf. Alec also worked on his inventions. Alec had an idea for a harmonic telegraph. This machine could send several messages at once across a telegraph wire.

Alec brought his plans for the machine to an electrical shop. A worker there named Thomas Watson built Alec's first harmonic telegraph in 1875. Thomas became Alec's assistant.

Alec moved to Boston in 1871 to teach students who were deaf and work on his inventions.

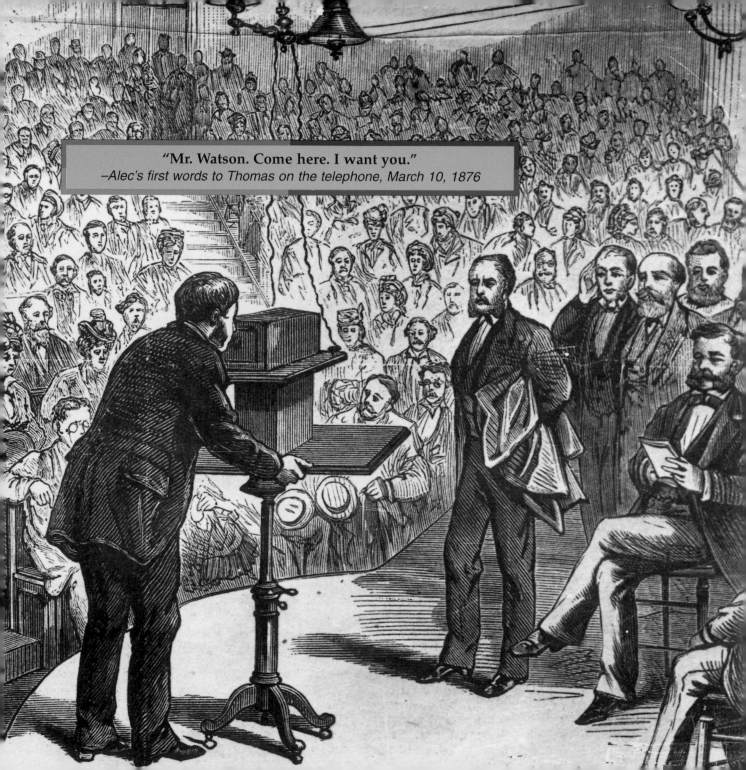

"Mr. Watson. Come here. I want you."
–Alec's first words to Thomas on the telephone, March 10, 1876

The Telephone

In 1875, Alec began to experiment with thin steel reeds. The reeds produced a tone when they vibrated. Alec and Thomas connected the reeds to an electrical wire. They tried to send tones across the wire. But they had little success.

On June 2, 1875, Thomas plucked at a reed. In the next room, Alec heard a faint twanging sound. The next day, Alec and Thomas strung a longer wire. The wire reached from the attic to the ground floor of the electrical shop.

In the attic, Alec spoke into a mouthpiece. Thomas heard Alec's voice from the ground floor. But he could not hear the individual words.

On March 10, 1876, Thomas heard Alec speak clearly over the wire. On October 6, they talked back and forth to each other. This was the first time two people talked on the telephone.

Alec and Thomas showed scientists how the telephone worked. They also showed the telephone to people who might buy one.

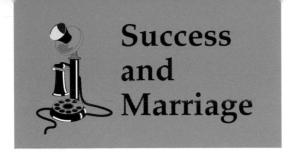

Success and Marriage

Alec met Mabel Hubbard when she became his student in 1873. She was 16 years old. Mabel had been deaf since the age of five. Her parents wanted Alec to help her speak more clearly.

Alec and Mabel became good friends. By 1876, Alec and Mabel knew they wanted to marry. But they decided to wait. Alec wanted to have enough money to support a family.

Hundreds of people were using telephones by the late 1870s. Many more people wanted to own telephones. To meet this need, Alec and several partners formed Bell Telephone Company.

On July 11, 1877, Alec and Mabel married. Alec gave Mabel most of his shares in the telephone company. This wedding gift made Mabel an owner of the business. Today, the company Alec helped begin is known as AT&T.

Alec and Mabel married in 1877. They had two daughters, Elsie May (left) and Marian (right).

Lifelong Inventor

The telephone made Alec famous and wealthy. But he kept working.

Important events inspired some of Alec's inventions. In 1881, President James A. Garfield was shot. Doctors could not find the bullets in the president's body.

Alec invented an electric probe to help doctors. The probe could locate pieces of metal inside human bodies. President Garfield died. But doctors used the probe for the next 20 years. The probe helped save many lives.

Mabel gave birth to a baby boy in 1881. The baby had trouble breathing and died within a few hours. Alec wanted to help cure breathing problems.

He invented a vacuum jacket that forced air into and out of the lungs. Many years later, scientists perfected the device and saved many lives.

Alec made the first telephone call on a telephone line that ran from New York to Chicago.

"Do not keep forever on the public road, going only where others have gone, and following one after the other like a flock of sheep. Leave the beaten track occasionally and dive into the woods. Every time you do so you will be certain to find something that you have never seen before."
—Alec in a speech to graduates of the
Friends School in Washington, D.C., 1914

Later Years

In 1886, Alec bought property in Nova Scotia, Canada. He continued his experiments there. Alec built a hydrofoil. This boat traveled across water on a cushion of air. In 1919, one of his hydrofoils reached 71 miles (114 kilometers) per hour. Alec's hydrofoil was the world's fastest boat for the next 10 years.

Alec never forgot the problems of people who were deaf. He started schools for students who were deaf. Alec also gave money to groups that helped educate people who were deaf.

In his later years, Alec suffered from diabetes. Diabetes is a disease in which the blood contains too much sugar. In the early 1900s, the disease could not be controlled.

Alec died on August 2, 1922. He was 75 years old. Alec's inventions changed the world. His work with people who were deaf changed many lives.

The U.S. Navy thought Alec's hydrofoil might be useful for fighting submarines. The navy gave Alec engines to use for the hydrofoil.

Fast Facts about Alexander Graham Bell

 Family and friends admired Alec's black eyes. But his eyes were sensitive to light. Alec had many headaches as a result.

 Alec became the National Geographic Society's president in 1898. He helped publish the society's magazine.

 All phones in the United States were turned off for one minute to honor Alec the day he was buried in Nova Scotia.

Dates in Alexander Graham Bell's life

1847—Born March 3 in Edinburgh, Scotland
1870—Moves to Canada with his family
1871—Moves to Boston to accept a job teaching students who are deaf
1875—Receives a patent for the harmonic telegraph
1876—Receives a patent for the telephone
1877—Forms Bell Telephone Company; marries Mabel Hubbard
1881—Son dies; invents vacuum jacket and electric probe
1883—Opens a school for deaf children in Washington, D.C.
1915—Helps open first coast-to-coast telephone line in the United States
1919—Builds a hydrofoil that sets the world speed record for boats
1922—Dies August 2 at age 75

Words to Know

climate (KLYE-mit)—the usual temperature and quality of the air; Alec's father, Melville, thought Scotland's climate was unhealthy.

communication (kuh-myoo-nuh-KAY-shuhn)—the sharing of ideas and information between two or more people

hydrofoil (HYE-druh-foil)—a boat that moves across the water on a cushion of air

invent (in-VENT)—to create a new thing or method; Alec's most famous invention was the telephone.

telegraph (TEL-uh-graf)—an instrument that uses electrical signals to send messages over wires

tuberculosis (tu-bur-kyuh-LOH-siss)—a lung disease that makes it hard for people to breathe

Read More

Davidson, Margaret. *The Story of Alexander Graham Bell: Inventor of the Telephone.* Famous Lives. Milwaukee: Gareth Stevens, 1997.

Fisher, Leonard Everett. *Alexander Graham Bell*. New York: Atheneum Books, 1998.

Parker, Steve. *Alexander Graham Bell and the Telephone*. Science Discoveries. New York: Chelsea House, 1995.

Useful Addresses

Alexander Graham Bell Association for the Deaf
3417 Volta Place NW
Washington, D.C. 20007-2778

Alexander Graham Bell National Historic Site
P.O. Box 159
Baddeck, NS BOE 1B0
Canada

Internet Sites

Alexander Graham Bell's Kids Page
http://bell.uccb.ns.ca/kids/kidsindex.htm
Brain Spin–Alexander Graham Bell
http://www.att.com:80/attlabs/brainspin/alexbell
Pasadena Kids Page–Alexander Graham Bell Links
http://www.e-znet.com/kids/AlexBellLinks.html

Index

AT&T, 5, 17
Bell, Alexander Melville, 7, 11
Bell, Edward, 7, 13
Bell, Mabel Hubbard, 17, 19
Bell, Melville, 7, 9, 13
Bell Telephone Company, 17
deaf, 11, 13, 17, 21
Edinburgh, Scotland, 7

electric probe, 19
harmonic telegraph, 13
hydrofoil, 5, 21
Nova Scotia, Canada, 21
speaking machine, 9
telephone, 5, 15, 17, 19
visible speech, 11
Watson, Thomas, 13, 15